D0710721

Who Works Here?

Car Dealership

by Lola M. Schaefer

Heinemann Library
Chicago, Illinois

© 2001 Reed Educational & Professional Publishing
Published by Heinemann Library,
an imprint of Reed Educational & Professional Publishing,
100 N. LaSalle, Suite 1010
Chicago, IL 60602
Customer Service 888-454-2279
Visit our website at www.heinemannlibrary.com

Designed by Wilkinson Design
Printed in Hong Kong

05 04 03 02 01
10 9 8 7 6 5 4 3 2 1

Library of Congress Cataloging-in-Publication Data
Schaefer, Lola M., 1950–
    Car dealership / by Lola M. Schaefer.
        p. cm. -- (Who works here?)
    Includes bibliographical references and index.
    ISBN 1-58810-123-1 (lb)
    1. Service stations--Juvenile literature. 2. Automobile dealers--Employees--Juvenile
    literature. [1. Automobile dealers. 2. Occupations.] I. Title.

    TL153 S33 2001
    629.222'068'8--dc21

                                                        00-058088

Acknowledgments
Photography by Phil Martin and Kimberly Saar.
Special thanks to Jim and Tom Kelley and all the workers at Tom Kelley Pontiac and GMC in Fort Wayne,
Indiana, and to workers everywhere who take pride in what they do.

Every effort has been made to contact copyright holders of any material reproduced in this book. Any omissions
will be rectified in subsequent printings if notice is given to the publisher.

Some words are shown in bold, **like this.**
You can find out what they mean by looking in the glossary.

Contents

What Is a Car Dealership?

A car dealership sells new and used cars to the public. The sales **department** displays the cars, trucks, and vans on outdoor lots and in the showroom. The people at the car dealership help **customers** find a car that makes them happy.

Most car dealerships also have a **service** department that repairs cars. Customers set up **appointments** for their cars. Everyone at a car dealership works hard to please the customers and offer good service.

Car dealerships have many shiny new cars to choose from.

This is the Kelley car dealership in Fort Wayne, Indiana. The map shows where the people in this book work. Many car dealerships in the United States look like this.

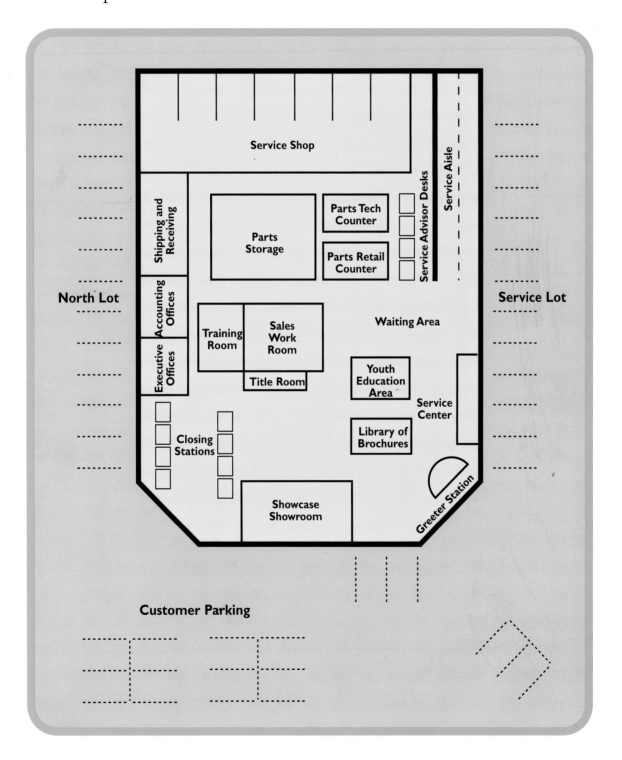

Owner

Jim is the owner of this car dealership. He and his staff are studying the new cars for next year.

The owner is responsible for all the **employees** and everything that happens at the car dealership. He or she is always looking for new ways to sell cars. The owner wants the price of a car to be the best one possible for the **customer**.

Most owners have worked at one or more car dealerships for many years. Many owners have had jobs in sales, service, and the parts **department**. They know how important it is to sell the customer a car at a fair price with good **service**.

The owner is welcoming a new employee to the car dealership.

General Manager

A general manager works with all the **departments** at the car dealership. He or she checks with the different managers to make sure the dealership is keeping **customers** happy and making money. A general manager **advertises** new car prices and special **services**.

Fred, a general manager, is collecting the sales information from the different department managers.

Fred, like most general managers, received special training for his job through a car company. He learned how to keep good money records and a wide **inventory** of cars. General managers go to **workshops** where they learn about new **equipment** and services.

Fred checks the price stickers on the cars in the lot.

Sales Consultant

A sales consultant finds the right new or used car for a **customer.** This person listens to the customers describe the kind of car they want. Since the sales consultant knows all of the **inventory,** he or she can offer the customer many choices.

Ed is a sales consultant. He is showing a customer the inside of a new car.

Sales consultants receive training at both the car companies and the car dealership. They drive all the new cars. They spend one week learning the **features** of each different car. New sales consultants learn all the steps in selling a car.

Ed watches as a customer signs a contract to buy a new car.

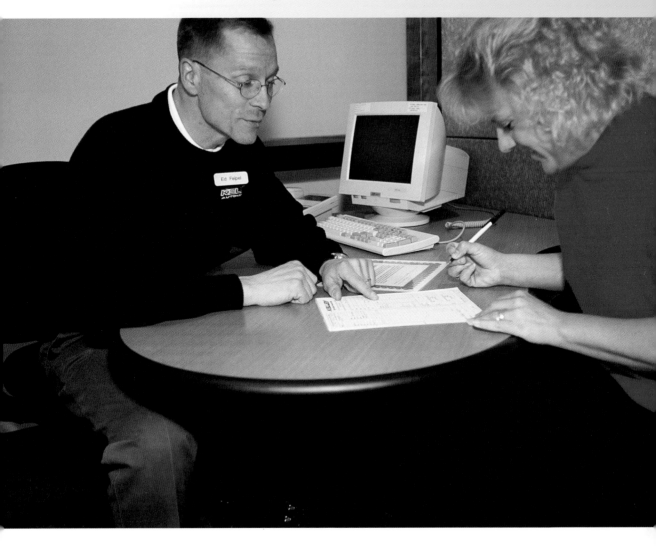

Title Clerk

A title clerk prepares the title after the sale of a car. A title is a legal document that shows who owns the car. A title clerk fills out the title for every car sold at the dealership. He or she then mails that information to the state government.

Jenny is a title clerk. She is recording information on a title.

Here, Jenny gives a title to a **customer**
before he drives away in his new car.

Title clerks train with another title clerk at the car
dealership. They learn to pay attention to detail. All of
their information needs to be recorded and filed
correctly. A title is an important paper to a car buyer.

Customer Relations Manager

Alice is a customer relations manager. Here, she is speaking with a customer through her headset.

A customer relations manager calls past **customers** of the dealership. He or she asks the customers if they are pleased with their cars and **service**. The customer relations manager then takes these comments to the general sales manager in order to improve customer service.

Customer relations managers work with all ages and types of people. They listen carefully to what customers say about the car dealership. Customer relations managers are friendly and polite. They help keep customers returning to the car dealership again and again.

Alice greets customers and offers them a place
to wait while their car is serviced.

Reservationist

Linda is a reservationist. She is making a service appointment for a customer with an engine problem.

A reservationist sets up **appointments** with **customers.** These appointments can be for repairs, **service,** or the **mobile** service van. A reservationist arranges for the mobile service technician and van to visit a customer's home to deliver or put in small parts.

Most reservationists receive customer service training at the car dealership. They learn how to speak on the telephone politely. They learn how to set up car repairs with other businesses when there is something the dealership cannot fix. Reservationists also receive computer training when needed.

Here, Linda visits the parts **department** to check if a customer's radio is ready to be picked up.

Service Advisor

The **customer** informs a service advisor what problems his or her car is having. The service advisor tells the customer about the repairs or **service** the car needs. The service advisor then records the problem for the technician and makes sure the car is fixed correctly on the first visit.

Steve is a service advisor at a car dealership. He is recording the problems a customer is having with his engine.

Here, the service advisor shows a customer that his car seat has been repaired.

To become a service advisor, a person must know how a car works. Service advisors receive training from both car companies and the car dealership. Part of that training is learning how to work well with people and use the computers.

Technician

A technician repairs cars brought into the service **department**. First, he or she connects a small computer to the car. The technician's computer tells him or her what needs to be repaired.

Using a hand-held computer, this technician learns that the car has a problem in the cooling system.

Brian, a technician, is fixing the air-conditioning system on this car.

Technicians usually go to training classes for 2-3 weeks for each skill they learn. Some technicians continue training to become master technicians. All technicians must pass a national test to be **certified**. Certified technicians work carefully so the customer can drive a safe car.

Using Service Technology

The Super Service Advisor is an **electronic** notepad with an **antenna**. A service advisor writes the repairs a car needs on the notepad. That information is sent directly into the service computer system through the antenna.

The pen on the notepad works like a mouse and keyboard on a computer. The service advisor can write or enter information with the pen.

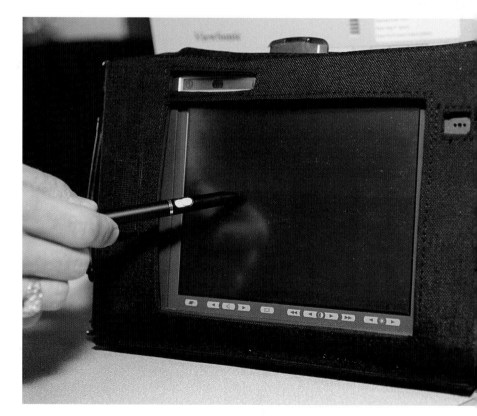

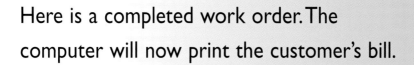

Here is a completed work order. The computer will now print the customer's bill.

The service computer system takes the information from the notepad and sends it to every service computer. All service advisors and technicians can look at the work order on a **monitor**. When the job is completed, the final charges are added.

Parts Manager

Rod is a parts manager at a car dealership.
He is counting oil pipes before placing an order.

A parts manager is responsible for everything in the parts **department**. This person keeps track of parts at the dealership and orders car parts they need at least once a day. A parts manager takes orders from **customers** at the counter and also trains new **employees**.

Rod, like other parts managers, trained for his job at the car company. He learned how to keep a full supply of parts and check on customer orders. It is important for parts managers to keep track of the money that goes in and out of their department every day.

Here, Rod places an order to the car company on his computer.

Car Porter

A car porter greets service **customers** at their cars in the service bay. He or she asks for their names and finds the paperwork in a file. The car porter gives the paperwork to a service advisor and waits with the customers.

John is a car porter. He is placing the customer's paperwork on a service advisor's desk.

This car porter is placing a free car wash sticker on a customer's car.

Car porters usually have ten weeks of customer service training. They learn how to keep customers calm and happy while waiting for the service advisor. Later, when a customer returns for his or her car, John drives the repaired car back to the service bay.

Courtesy Van Driver

A courtesy van driver transports service **customers** to work or home from the car dealership. Later in the day, this person will pick up the customers at work or home and bring them back to the car dealership for their cars.

Nate is a courtesy van driver. Each morning he receives customer pick-up information from the car dealership.

Nate is driving this customer to work while her car brakes are repaired.

Courtesy van drivers are hired because they are good drivers. Car dealerships want to transport their customers safely. Courtesy van drivers fill their vans with gas every day. In the morning, they clean their vans inside and out. Customers like the helpful service of courtesy van drivers.

Glossary

advertise tell many people about a product in a way that makes them want to buy it

antenna wire that sends or receives radio and television signals

appointment time agreed for a meeting

certified licensed to perform a job after passing a test

communication sharing of information, ideas, or feelings with another person by talking, writing, or drawing

contract document that shows an agreement that is supported by the law

customer person who shops and buys in a store or business

department part of a business or organization that has a particular job or purpose

electronic devices that are powered by small amounts of electricity

employee person who works for someone else and is paid to do so

equipment tools and machines used for a special purpose

feature important part or quality of something

inventory all the items on hand for sale in a store

mobile able to move

monitor TV screen used with a computer

organize plan and run an event

service repairing of a car·or an appliance

work order written record of the repairs needed

More Books to Read

Boraas, Tracey. *Automotive Master Mechanic.* Mankato, Minn.: Capstone Press, Inc., 2000.

Florian, Douglas. *An Auto Mechanic.* New York, N.Y.: Morrow Avon, 1994.

An older reader can help you with this one:

Eberts, Marjorie, and Martha Eberts. *Cars.* Lincolnwood, Ill.: NTC Contemporary Publishing Company, 1995.

Index

JONAS SALK SCHOOL
2950 HURLEY WAY
SACRAMENTO, CA 95864